Texaplex is dedicated to my wife, Dana, whom I love and adore, cherish, and respect.

No part of this publication may be reproduced, stored in a retrieval system or transmitted in any form or by any means, electronic, mechanical, photocopying, recording or otherwise, without prior permission of Texaplex Media, LLC. For information regarding permission, please write to Texaplex Media, LLC., 17734 Preston Road, Suite 100 Dallas, TX 75252

Copyright © 2015 by David Winans

All Rights Reserved

Texaplex is a trademark of David Winans.

WELCOME TO TEXAS

Many have said I might be responsible for a good percentage of the 2,000 people moving to Texas every day. Much credit for the crushing wave of people and companies moving to the Lone Star State is given to my Texaplex project. It was six years ago that I coined the word Texaplex and created a 7 minute video about Texas that quickly went viral. The Texas Governor's office shared the Texaplex video, welcoming the world to our great state. It has been mentioned on NBC, *The Economist*, *Newsweek*, and many other world publications. However, I can't take the credit.

The fact is, Texas is the best place in America to live, work and raise a family. Texas boasts a pro-growth tax policy offering no state income tax, a low tax burden for businesses, and sensible laws and regulations. This is drawing an increasing number of American firms seeking to relocate to Texas. The two primary drivers bringing big numbers to Texas: jobs and affordable housing. The Lone Star State is blessed with both.

Texas is America's new land of opportunity.

TEXAPLEX

America's New Land of Opportunity

David Winans

Texaplex Media, LLC

THE TEXAPLEX

is the triangular region in Texas anchored by the metropolitan areas of Dallas–Fort Worth, Houston, Austin, and San Antonio, where nearly 75% of the population lives. Highways form the sides of the triangle, each one averaging 230 miles in length. The Texaplex contains less than a quarter of the land mass of Texas.

Texans don't lie... We just think bigger.
–Unknown Texan

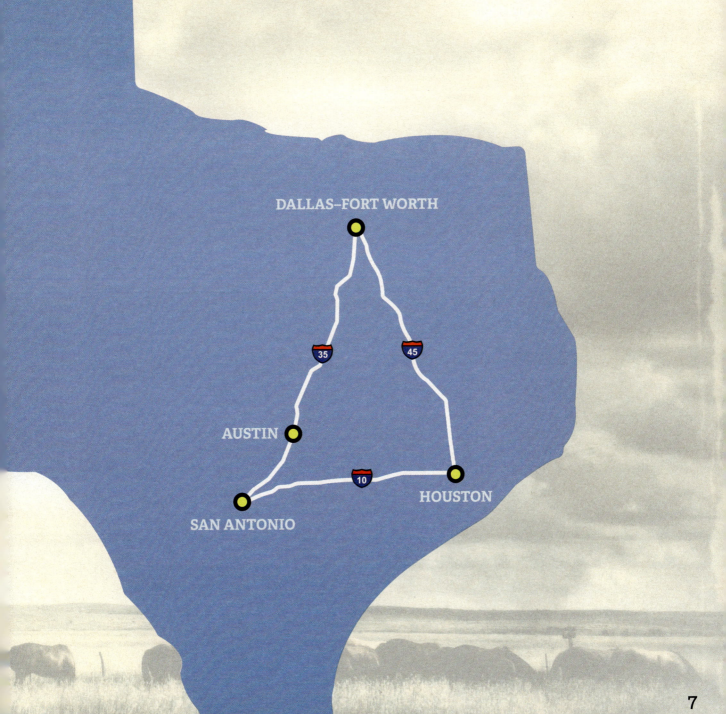

How did Texas, and more specifically the Texaplex, become the perfect storm for growth and opportunity? Looking back at the population growth in the United States sheds some light on this question.

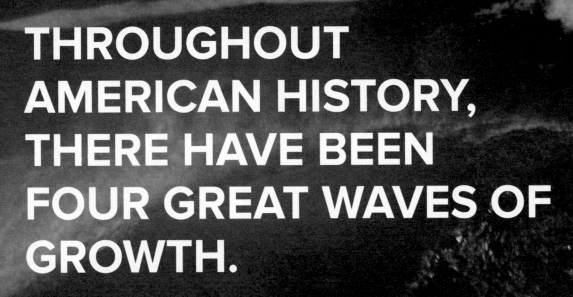

THROUGHOUT AMERICAN HISTORY, THERE HAVE BEEN FOUR GREAT WAVES OF GROWTH.

"Four Waves of Growth" is credited to Houstonian Tory Gattis, a social systems architect.

4 WAVES OF GROWTH

WAVE 1

America's Original Land of Opportunity

NEW-YORK

The first wave began in Boston, New York City, Philadelphia, Baltimore, and the Washington, DC corridor. This was America's original land of opportunity, industry, wealth, and power. New York City was the big winner; Washington DC and Boston still do quite well.

4 WAVES OF GROWTH

WAVE 2

The Rise of the Agricultural and Industrial Midwest

The second historical wave was the rise of the agricultural and industrial Midwest, including Chicago, Detroit, Pittsburgh, Cleveland, and St Louis. The fall of this region was a hard one as manufacturing moved abroad, but Chicago still stands as a world-class city.

4 WAVES OF GROWTH

WAVE 3

The Great Westward Migration

The third wave was the great westward migration, mostly focused on California, but with ancillary growth in adjacent and West Coast states. This migration started well before World War II, but really took off after the war. It produced two top-tier mega-metros—Los Angeles and the San Francisco Bay area—and several successful second-tier cities like Seattle, San Diego, Las Vegas, and Phoenix.

4 WAVES OF GROWTH

WAVE 4

The Texaplex and the New South

The fourth wave is increasingly clear and follows the same California model of a single focus mega-state and an ancillary region—the Texaplex and the new south.

These waves are not clearly distinct but overlap each other. As one region matures and starts to level off, the next region starts its growth wave. That's the situation now as California shows clear signs of having peaked with outmigration on the rise, high cost of living, regulatory burdens, and a dysfunctional government.

Just as California had its pre-war growth surge, Texas had its first real growth wave in the 20th century post-Spindletop oil boom. California had the dust bowl migration of the 30s, and Texas had the oil boom migration of the 70s. But the real super-surge has become clearer in the new century as California hands off the baton to Texas. This growth wave really covers much of the South, but Texas is the 800 lb gorilla vs. states like Georgia and North Carolina, just as California dominates over Washington, Nevada, and Arizona. Texas even looms over Florida, which certainly has experienced incredible population growth to become the fourth-largest state, but has had considerably less success with building industry, wealth, and power. Florida's wealth—like that of Arizona—comes in part from people who built their wealth elsewhere but moved or bought a second home there. Neither place is home to as many Fortune 500 headquarters, an area where Texas has excelled.

If a man's from Texas, he'll tell you. If he's not, why embarrass him by asking?

–John Gunther
US Journalist

California had its agriculture and oil barons before WWII, but the real story there was the post-war rise of entertainment, defense, aerospace, biotech, trade, and technology industries. In a similar way, Texas' oil tycoons are just the tip of the coming surge of wealth and power in industries such as technology, health care, biotech, defense, transportation, aerospace, finance, telecom, and alternative energy in addition to traditional oil and gas.

The two great metro areas emerging from this new wave are Houston and Dallas–Fort Worth. They dominate the growth statistics in the latest census. These two metros now rank #4 and #5 in population behind NYC, Los Angeles, and Chicago. San Antonio is the 7th largest city in the United States, and Austin is one of the fastest growing cities in the country.

TEXA★QUOTE

I must say as to what I have seen of Texas, it is the garden spot of the world. The best land and the best prospects for health I ever saw is here, and I do believe it is a fortune to any man to come here.

–David Crockett
Alamo Hero

If you stand back and look at the big picture, those living in the Texaplex are part of a great historical wave that's just starting to take off, the same as living in Chicago at the turn of the 19th Century or California after WWII.

Let's take a closer look at why everyone is talking about Texas.

TEXAS IS BIG

If the entire 7 billion population of the world moved to Texas, there would be 1,100 square feet of space for every man, woman, and child on the planet. That's more space than what New York City dwellers are already used to.

TEXA★QUOTE

I love Texas because Texas is future-oriented, because Texans think anything is possible. Texans think big.

–Phil Gramm
US Senator

IF TEXAS WERE A COUNTRY, IT WOULD BE THE 14th LARGEST ECONOMY IN THE WORLD.*

According to Forbes, if Texas were a nation it would rank as the 6th largest oil producer in the world, exceeding 3 million barrels of oil production a day.

* as ranked by GDP

TEXAS IS 268,820 SQUARE MILES; THAT IS 7.4% OF THE NATION.

It's bigger than New England, New York, Pennsylvania, Ohio, and Illinois... COMBINED!

The current population of Texas is 27 million, not including 16 million cattle.

The King Ranch has over 800,000 acres and is larger than the entire state of Rhode Island.

Texas is still a last frontier. It is part of the United States where the traditional virtues are still operating. In short, a piece of living history.

–John C. B. Richmond
  Author

With over 130 million acres of farmland, Texas has more than double the total amount of farmland of any other state.

But contrary to popular belief, Texas is not an open range full of cowboys and horses.

IN FACT, TEXAS IS A BUDDING AND MODERN URBAN MEGALOPOLIS.

(We prefer Texaplex)

No matter how far we may wander, Texas lingers with us, coloring our perceptions of the world.

–Elmer Kelto
Author

OF THE ELEVEN MOST POPULATED CITIES IN THE US,

FOUR ARE IN THE TEXAPLEX

1. New York City
2. Los Angeles
3. Chicago
4. **Houston**
5. Philadelphia
6. Phoenix
7. **San Antonio**
8. San Diego
9. **Dallas**
10. San Jose
11. **Austin**

Both the Dallas–Fort Worth metro area and the Houston metro area **individually** have larger populations than 33 US states.

Texas is a leader in alternative energy sources, producing the most wind power of any state.

4 JUMBO JETS EVERY DAY

As big as Texas is, believe it or not, it's getting even bigger.

Texas is growing by over 2,000 people a day.

That's like four jumbo jets landing in the middle of Texas every morning and no one has a return ticket. Texas is now their home.

LOOK AT THE STAGGERING GROWTH

Texas Population Projected Growth

	Current	2030	2050
Austin	2 million	3 million	5.3 million
DFW	7 million	10 million	16.7 million
Houston	6.6 million	9.3 million	14.4 million
San Antonio	2.4 million	3.2 million	4.2 million

Source: Texas State Demographer's Office

This population increase over the next 35 years is like adding to the current Texaplex area:

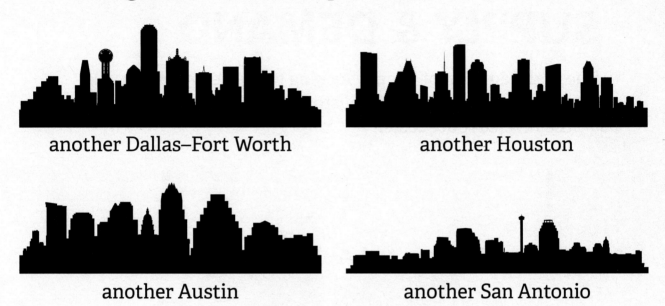

another Dallas–Fort Worth

another Houston

another Austin

another San Antonio

...and throw in a Los Angeles

LET'S TALK ABOUT SUPPLY & DEMAND

Due to the amount of people flocking to the Texaplex, a truck rental from Los Angeles to Houston costs over double what the reverse route costs.

Houston to LA: $1,031

LA to Houston: $2,458

Truck Rental Prices at UHAUL.com

WHY ARE PEOPLE AND BUSINESSES MOVING TO TEXAS?

One idea... Jobs.

Texas leads the nation in job growth—and they're good jobs. Since 2000, Texas has created 2.1 million jobs; that's 30 percent of all the jobs created in America.

TEXAS HAS BEEN THE TOP EXPORTING STATE 14 YEARS IN A ROW

Texas grosses more in exports than California and New York combined.

Texas just surpassed California as the top tech supplier of semiconductors, telecommunication devices, computers, and other electronics.

54 FORTUNE 500 COMPANIES IN TEXAS

With no state income tax, and no tax on goods in transit, it's no wonder Texas is home to over 52 Fortune 500 companies.

 Texas: A perfect storm of opportunity and growth.
–David Winans

TEXAS IS BUSINESS FRIENDLY

Texas has always been business friendly. The world's largest operator of convenience stores (with over 50,000 outlets) started with one store in Texas in 1927.

FORBES' BEST BUY CITIES

Where to invest in housing in 2015

1. Austin
3. Houston
5. Dallas
6. San Antonio
10. Fort Worth

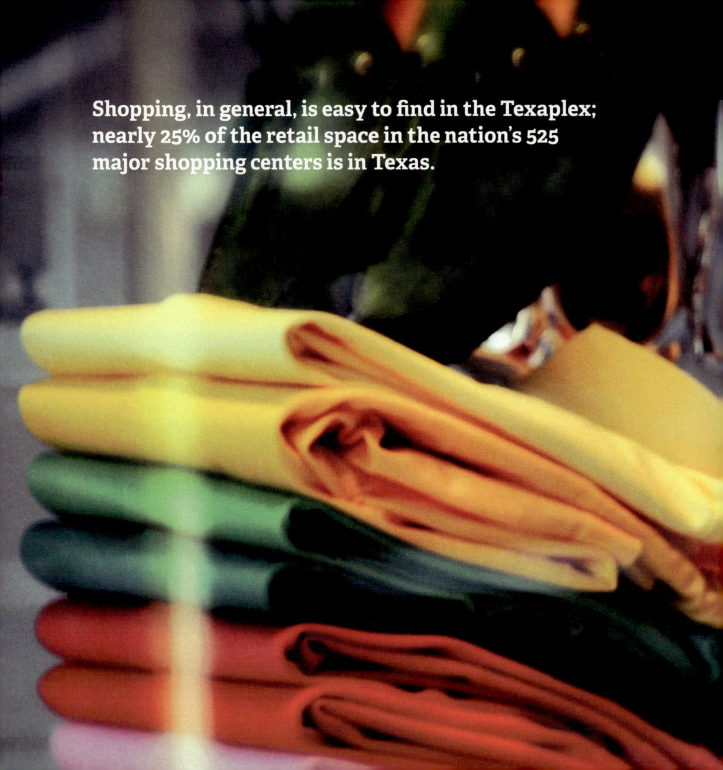

Shopping, in general, is easy to find in the Texaplex; nearly 25% of the retail space in the nation's 525 major shopping centers is in Texas.

TEXAPLEX SPORTS

The Friday night lights are a serious affair in the Texaplex, but it's far from the only game in town. Teams from all major professional sports are represented in the Texaplex, including NFL, MLB, NBA, NHL, and MLS teams.

- DALLAS COWBOYS
- HOUSTON ASTROS
- DALLAS MAVERICKS
- HOUSTON DYNAMO
- DALLAS STARS
- SAN ANTONIO SPURS
- FC DALLAS
- HOUSTON TEXANS
- TEXAS RANGERS
- HOUSTON ROCKETS

Texas is a state of mind. Texas is an obsession. Above all, Texas is a nation in every sense of the word.

–John Steinbeck
Author

So, what does all this mean for those who call the Lone Star State home?

Opportunity.

Opportunity for individuals, families, and businesses. More jobs, more commerce, and more real estate opportunities.

The Texaplex is a hotbed of opportunity and growth. Its size, population, growth, economy, and culture are all excellent reasons to believe that Texas will continue to shine as a Lone Star.

The Texaplex offers explosive potential. It's going to be a Lone Star Boom!

Austin

Austin, the capital of Texas, is the 11th largest city in the country and is within 200 miles of four of the largest cities in the US: Houston, San Antonio, Dallas, and Fort Worth.

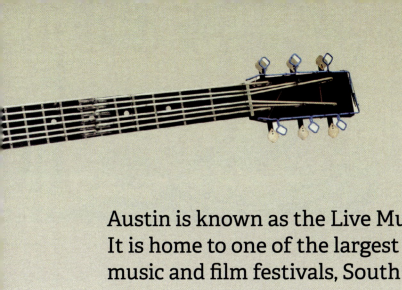

Austin is known as the Live Music Capital of the World. It is home to one of the largest and most important music and film festivals, South by Southwest (SXSW).

The people of Austin reflect a friendly, accepting culture of artistic and individual expression.

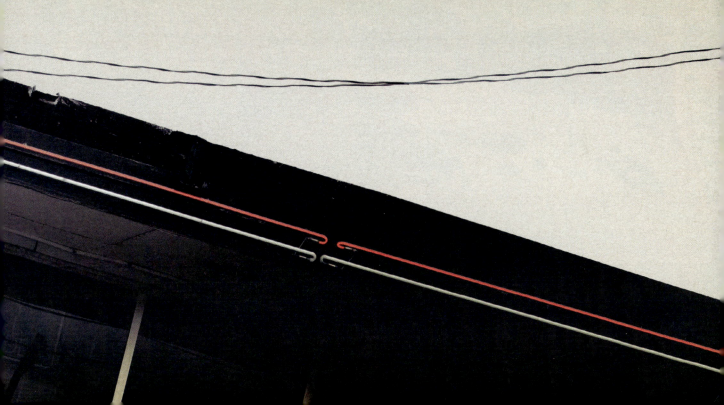

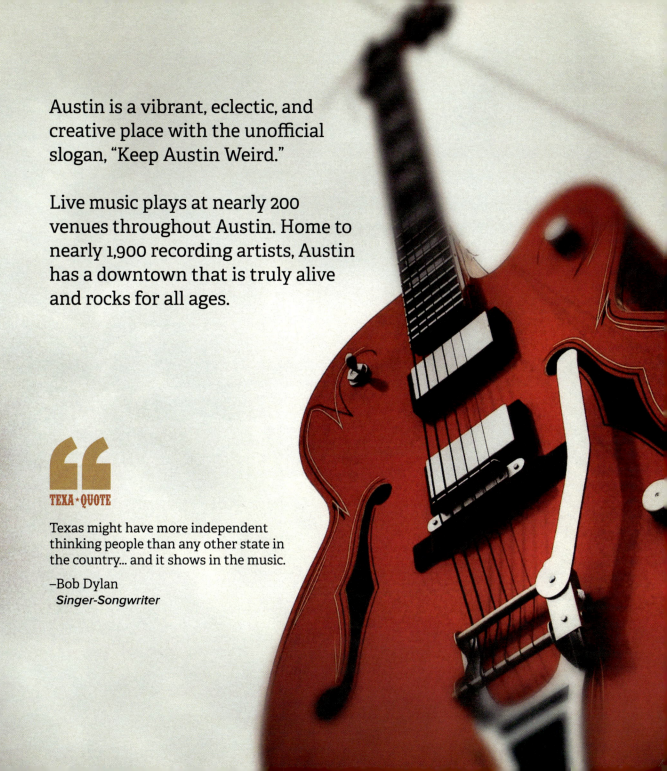

Austin is a vibrant, eclectic, and creative place with the unofficial slogan, "Keep Austin Weird."

Live music plays at nearly 200 venues throughout Austin. Home to nearly 1,900 recording artists, Austin has a downtown that is truly alive and rocks for all ages.

TEXA★QUOTE

Texas might have more independent thinking people than any other state in the country... and it shows in the music.

–Bob Dylan
Singer-Songwriter

Austin has 300 days of sunshine annually. Outdoor recreational opportunities abound with over 200 parks, including the 360 acre Zilker Park and a 10.1 mile hike and bike trail around Lady Bird Johnson Lake.

Like to swim? The Highland Lakes chain runs through the middle of Austin and there are seven lakes with over 750 miles of fresh water shoreline within an hour of downtown. The refreshing Barton Springs Pool welcomes swimmers to 68-degree, spring-fed waters year round.

The city is considered one of the most bike-friendly cities in America.

Newsday calls Austin a foodie and family friendly destination, located at the hub of more than 20 wineries on the Texas Wine Trail. Austin is home to the world headquarters for Whole Foods Market.

According to Liveability.com, Austin is the 3rd best city in America for new college graduates.

Along with Houston, Austin consistently ranks as one of the top cities in Forbes' annual list of America's fastest growing cities.

Travel & Leisure ranks Austin 3rd in "America's Techiest Cities."

AUSTIN IS ONE OF THE HOTTEST STARTUP CITIES ACCORDING TO RJ METRICS.

The proliferation of technology companies has led to the region's nickname, "the Silicon Hills." High-tech companies with operations in the Austin area include:

3M, Apple, Hewlett-Packard, Google, Dell, Visa, Qualcomm, AMD, Applied Materials, Cirrus Logic, ARM Holdings, Cisco Systems, Electronic Arts, Flextronics, Facebook, eBay/PayPal, Bioware, Blizzard Entertainment, Hoover's, Intel Corporation, National Instruments, Rackspace, RetailMeNot, Rooster Teeth, Spansion, Buffalo Technology, Silicon Laboratories, Xerox, Oracle, Hostgator, Samsung Group, HomeAway, and United Devices.

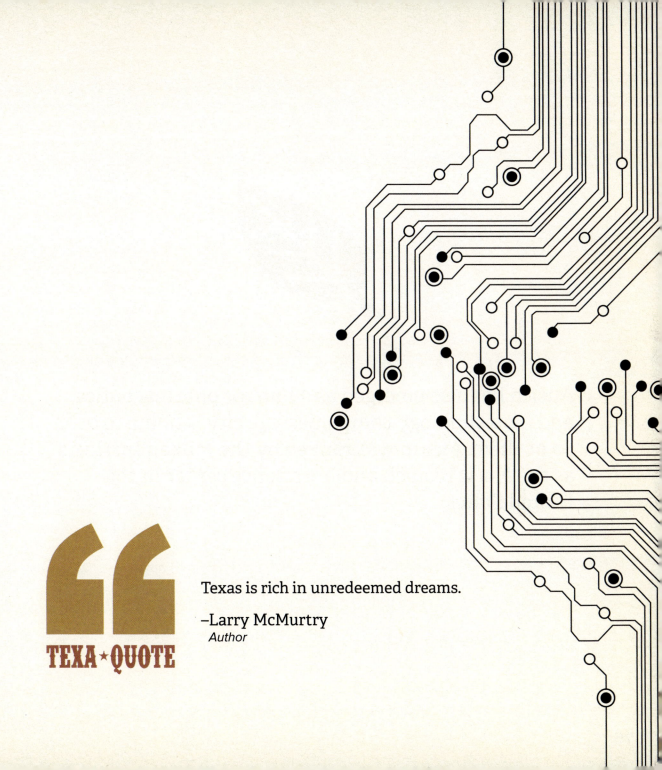

" "

TEXA★QUOTE

Texas is rich in unredeemed dreams.

–Larry McMurtry
  Author

Austin has also emerged as a hub for pharmaceutical and biotechnology companies; the city is home to over 80 of them. Austin was ranked by the Milken Institute as the No. 12 biotech and life science center in the United States.

MovieMaker Magazine ranks Austin #1 in the top 10 cities to be a moviemaker.

Austin is the largest city in the United States without a club in a major professional sports league... but who cares? Austin has the University of Texas.

Hook 'em Horns!

Dallas–Fort Worth

Dallas–Fort Worth is one of the fastest-growing metropolitan areas in the nation.

With a growing population of over 7 million, it's the 4th largest metro area in the country and the largest in the Texaplex!

At the heart of Dallas–Fort Worth, also known as The Metroplex, is a massive airport, surrounded by Fort Worth in the West, Dallas in the East, and over 200 suburban cities!

DALLAS/FORT WORTH INTERNATIONAL AIRPORT

Even the DFW International Airport is larger than Manhattan.

Whether your destination is heaven or hell, you always have to change planes in Dallas.

–Kinky Friedman
  Author

This isn't just a growth spurt. The Dallas–Fort Worth Metroplex has consistently added more than 300 residents per day... for the last 30 years.

Dallas–Fort Worth is built on innovation and the entrepreneurial spirit fostered since the area was founded in the mid-1800s.

Today, Dallas–Fort Worth leads the nation with the most shopping centers per capita.

The first convenience store in the nation was opened in Dallas–Fort Worth in the 1920s.

That one small store became the global corporation known as 7-Eleven.

Resident Don Wetzel invented the ATM.

The frozen margarita machine was invented by Dallas–Fort Worth restaurateur Mariano Martinez.

But no invention can match what came out of Dallas–Fort Worth in 1958. The first integrated circuit—what would one day become the microchip—was invented by Jack Kilby at Texas Instruments. He was just one of the Dallas–Fort Worth residents who changed our world forever.

WITH THIS MUCH ENTREPRENEURIAL SPIRIT AND A "CAN DO" ATTITUDE, IT'S NO WONDER THAT DALLAS–FORT WORTH IS THE FASTEST-GROWING METROPOLITAN AREA IN THE NATION, ADDING OVER 145,000 RESIDENTS IN THE LAST YEAR ALONE.

With over 7 million residents, it's the fourth-largest metro in the US, behind only New York City, Los Angeles, and Chicago.

That's more residents than 36 states!

And the numbers keep rising: by 2030, the Metroplex is estimated to grow to 10 million residents.

The Dallas–Fort Worth area encompasses 9,286 square miles, making it larger than Rhode Island and Connecticut combined.

DALLAS–FORT WORTH MEANS BUSINESS

Dallas–Fort Worth was selected by *Inc. Magazine* as one of the best metropolitan areas for entrepreneurs and is home to eighteen Fortune 500 companies.

There are over 145,000 businesses in the Dallas–Fort Worth area and more than 1,500 regional and corporate headquarters.

Twenty-five billionaires call The Metroplex home—only three other cities in the world have more.

Texas is neither southern nor western. Texas is Texas.

–William Blakley
  US Senator

The Metroplex is known as the nation's largest inland port. It has the second largest number of freeway miles per capita in the nation. Within 24 hours, truck drivers can reach 37 percent of the nation's population, and in 48 hours they can reach 93 percent.

 You can take the girl out of Texas but not the Texas out of the girl, and ultimately, not the girl out of Texas.

–Janine Turner
Actor

The Metroplex's geographical location gives it a superior advantage.

It's location in the Central Time Zone extends the work day for companies doing business on both coasts.

With no state income tax and no tax on goods in transit, it's no wonder Dallas–Fort Worth is such an important transportation hub of highways, railways, and airways.

DFW International Airport has a total area of thirty square miles, making it larger than Manhattan. It's the largest airport in Texas and the second largest in the US.

In terms of aircraft movement, it is the third busiest airport in the world. In terms of passenger traffic, it is the ninth busiest worldwide.

The Dallas–Fort Worth Metroplex is a great place to live, learn, and have fun!

It provides residents with state-of-the-art care at any of its 90 hospitals.

Collectively, its private and public universities enroll over 297,000 students.

For golfers, Dallas–Fort Worth boasts over 200 courses from which to choose.

There are over 60 lakes and reservoirs within 100 miles of Dallas–Fort Worth.

Texas is the crossroads of the world. Everything here is big.
–Bobby Lee
　Author

The State Fair of Texas, known for its famous fried treats, is the largest annual state fair in the nation.

The Metroplex is home to more restaurants per capita than New York City.

Both Dallas and Fort Worth are home to growing and well-respected arts districts, and the Metroplex is quickly becoming known as a film industry hot spot.

Housing costs are significantly lower than other US cities of its size.

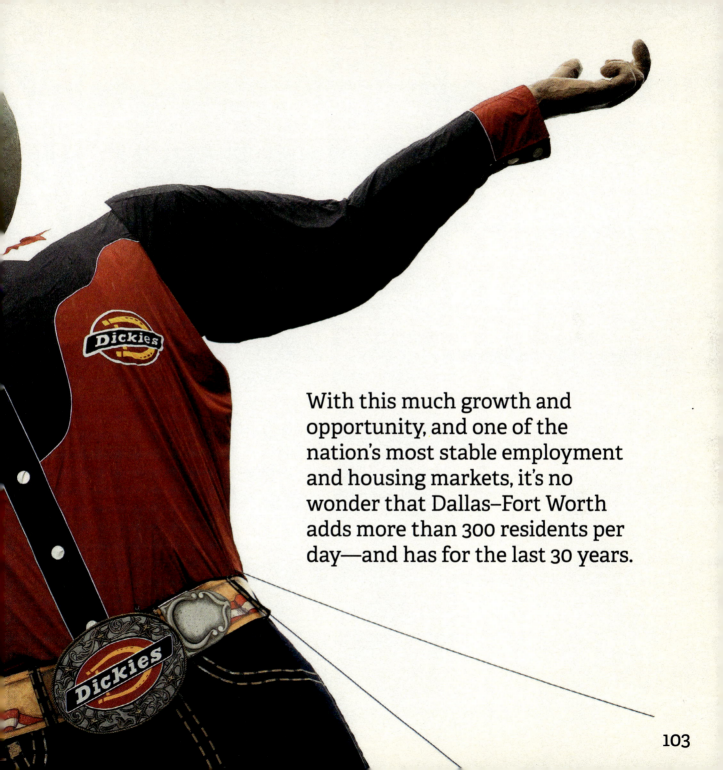

With this much growth and opportunity, and one of the nation's most stable employment and housing markets, it's no wonder that Dallas–Fort Worth adds more than 300 residents per day—and has for the last 30 years.

Houston

Houston is many things. It's diverse, progressive, economically thriving, and entirely affordable.

Houston is big! With a growing population of 6.6 million, the Houston metro area has more residents than 33 states. It is the largest city in the southern United States and the 4th largest overall.

There's plenty of room for all this growth: the 600 square miles that make up the city of Houston could contain the cities of New York, Washington, DC, Boston, San Francisco, Seattle, Minneapolis, and Miami.

If Houston were an independent nation—and don't think they haven't considered it—it would rank as the world's 30th largest economy.

I am forced to conclude that God made Texas on his day off, for pure entertainment, just to prove that all that diversity could be crammed into one section of earth by a really top hand.

–Mary Lasswell
Author

This massive population and economy supports the 6th largest airport system in the world, serving more than 51 million passengers each year.

The Texas Medical Center in Houston is the largest medical center complex in the world. 5 million patients each year visit the Center, which boasts over 20 million square feet of space and employs more than 50,000 people. The MD Anderson Cancer Center is the US News & World Report's #2 cancer treatment facility in the US.

With the local economic impact at 10 billion dollars, the expanding healthcare economy will likely be a boom for the Center and the city.

With more than 5,000 energy-related firms, Houston is known by many as the Energy Capital of the World. But it's not all just big oil. Houston's focus on energy has resulted in a progressive, modern approach to energy creation. 32% of the city's electricity load is purchased from wind energy.

Houston's progressive attitude may have something to do with the fact that the city is home to the nation's third-largest concentration of consular offices, representing 86 countries.

More than 90 languages are spoken throughout the Houston area, revealing the city population's various ethnic and religious backgrounds, as well as a growing international community.

The weather is warm—it drops below freezing only 18 days a year. All this sunshine means you can work on your golf game 365 days a year at one of more than 165 public and private golf courses.

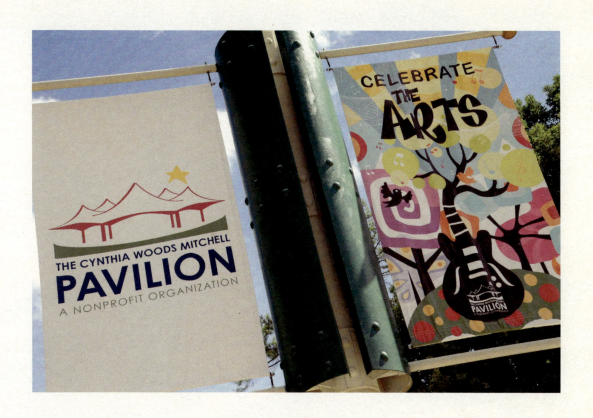

But if sports aren't your thing, there's still plenty to do. Houston's 17-block theater district is second only to New York City. Home to eight performing arts organizations with more than 12,000 seats, Houston offers world-class, year-round entertainment in all major performing arts.

If you'd rather spend more time outdoors, you'll be happy to know that Houston ranks first among the nation's most populous cities in total acreage of parkland. Boat enthusiasts find plenty to love in Houston, as well.

Located 50 miles from the Gulf of Mexico, and just 30 minutes from the 2,000 acre Clear Lake destination, it's no wonder Houston has the third-largest pleasure boat harbor in the United States.

Houston is a city of incredible opportunity, where great things continue to happen. Houston is a city of infinite possibilities.

Houston is, without a doubt, the weirdest, most entertaining city in Texas, consisting as it does of subtropical forest, life in the fast lane, a layer of oil, cowboys and spacemen.

–Texas Tourism Guide

San Antonio

San Antonio is the 7th most populous city in the nation and the 2nd most populous in the state of Texas.

26 million tourists visit San Antonio and the New Braunfels area each year, and many of them decided to stay and make it their home.

San Antonio was the fastest growing city of the top 10 largest US cities from 2000–2010.

San Antonio will add nearly 2 million residents in the next 35 years.

The San Antonio Riverwalk, also known as the Paseo del Rio, is the largest urban ecosystem in the nation.

San Antonio and the New Braunfels area boasts three lakes and the world-recognized Schlitterbahn—the best water park in the world.

 I think Texans have more fun than the rest of the world.
–Tommy Tune
Choreographer

San Antonio and the New Braunfels area has a strong military presence with Joint Base San Antonio (JBSA).

The defense industry employs 89,000 people with an economic impact of over $10 billion a year.

San Antonio is home to USAA and its 286 acre campus.

The University of Texas at San Antonio is the 4th largest university in the state of Texas, home to an enormous medical community including UT's medical and dental schools.

San Antonio is also home to the South Texas Veterans Health Care System, a huge VA hospital complex.

All four branches of the military do all of their field medical training in San Antonio.

San Antonio and the New Braunfels area hosts both a PGA and Sr. PGA tournament every year.

 If you've ever driven across Texas, you know how different one area of the state can be from another. Take El Paso. It looks as much like Dallas as I look like Jack Nicklaus.

–Lee Trevino
Pro Golfer

Fiesta Texas is an annual spring festival with origins dating back to the late 19th century. Each year more than 3 million people participate in Fiesta. On a national scale, Fiesta Texas is second in size only to the Tournament of Roses parade.

The San Antonio Stock Show and Rodeo is one of the largest in the country. The annual event takes place for three weeks in February.

In 1932, CE Doolin bought a recipe for fried corn chips from a Mexican man in San Antonio for $100. Doolin started canning chips known as Fritos.

The Outlets in San Marcos, near San Antonio, were voted "Third Best Place to Shop in the World" by ABC's *The View*.

The 250-acre Sea World San Antonio is the largest of the three Sea World parks.

The Alamodome has 65,000 seats. If lined up side-by-side, they would stretch 25 miles.

REMEMBER THE ALAMO

2.5 million people visit the sacred site each year. The Battle of the Alamo was a pivotal event in the Texas Revolution. Led by James Bowie and David Crockett, Texas defenders held on for 13 days before being defeated. Six weeks later, an army led by Sam Houston defeated the Mexican soldiers at the Battle of San Jacinto and Texas independence was won.

You may all go to hell, and I will go to Texas.
–David Crockett

DAVID WINANS

David Winans is a successful entrepreneur and real estate broker who coined the term and created the Texaplex Project. He grew up in California, but as the old saying goes, he got to Texas as fast as he could. An impassioned cheerleader for Texas, David created the Texaplex Project in an effort to share with the world what he's known for years; that Texas—and specifically the Texaplex region—is a perfect storm of opportunity and growth. For more information on David and the Texaplex Project, visit texaplex.com.

DAVID KOZLOWSKI

David Kozlowski is one of Texas' emerging photography superstars. Dave has a style that is fresh and creative.

A native of Pennsylvania, Dave moved to Texas in 2000 and has never looked back. His list of clients includes major corporations and well known universities. For more information about Dave and his photography, visit dallasphotoworks.com.